How   se

BATTERIES
NOT
INCLUDED

D A V I D   S E T T L E

Copyright © 2023 David Settle

All rights reserved. No part of this book may be reproduced, stored, or transmitted by any means—whether auditory, graphic, mechanical, or electronic—without written permission of both publisher and author, except in the case of brief excerpts used in critical articles and reviews. Unauthorized reproduction of any part of this work is illegal and is punishable by law.

CONTENTS

Foreword vii
Introduction – Tis' the Season for BATTERIES xi
    Disclaimer - WARNING! xiii

Battery #1 – FOCUS to Thrive 1
    Ready, AIM, Fire! 2
    Jack of All Trades, Master of None 7
        Reflections/Takeaways 13

Battery #2 – FREEDOM to Flourish 17
    FREE from Distractions 19
        Reflections/Takeaways 26
    FREE From Negative Habits 28
        Reflections/Takeaways 33
    Freedom from Doin' the Most - Prioritizing
    Purposeful Productivity 36
        A Parallel to Financial Wisdom 36
        Time: A Finite Treasure 37
        The Art of Prioritization 38
        Investing in Meaning 38
        The Mirage of Constant Activity 39
        The Vital Role of Delegation and Automation 40

- The Impact of Purposeful Productivity........................42
- Mindful Time Management................................43
- Breaking Free from the Excessive Hustle....................43
  - **Reflections/Takeaways**............................45
- FREE From Self-Doubt.......................................48
  - Subtract to Add: Creating Space for Growth..................48
  - Confronting Negative Self-Talk............................49
  - Set Realistic Goals..49
  - Seek Social Support.......................................50
  - Embrace Failure as a Learning Opportunity..................50
  - Practice Mindfulness and Self-Awareness...................51
  - Celebrate Achievements...................................51
  - Seek Professional Help When Needed......................52
  - **Reflections/Takeaways**............................53

Battery #3 – FAITH to fly!..................................57
- The visualizing power of belief............................59
- The limitless potential of belief...........................60
- Belief vs Hope...60
- Speak what you seek until you see what you said!..........62
  - **Reflections/Takeaways**............................63

Battery #4 – FORCE to Succeed...........................67
- Nothing works but work..................................68
- The law of motion.......................................68
- Embracing the Heat: From Good to Great..................70
- From Potential to Power: Harnessing the FORCE within to Forge Ahead.......................................72
  - **Reflections/Takeaways**............................74

Battery #5 – FUN The Fuel of Fulfillment 77
    The Science of Fun 78
    The Journey of Fun 79
    Live, Laugh, Succeed 79
    Action Steps. 80
        Find Your Joy. 80
        Celebrate Small 80
        Share Laughter. 80
        Embrace Play 81
        Reflections/Takeaways. 82

All Charged Up: Powering Your Purpose, Fueled by Focus, Faith, Freedom, Force, and Fun. 85

FOREWORD

BY KARL PHILLIPS

When I think about my dear friend David, one word consistently comes to mind – resilience. Over the course of more than a decade, I have witnessed David navigate through life's tumultuous waters, and not only survive but thrive. He has been a remarkable example of someone who plays the hand life deals him with unwavering determination, a bright smile, and an inspiring sense of purpose.

From his early days as a DJ, setting dance floors on fire, to the man he is today, striving to change the world one person at a time, I have had the privilege of observing his remarkable evolution. The journey that David embarked upon, transforming himself from a master of beats to a master of life, is one that has left an indelible mark on me.

In "Batteries Not Included," David takes us on an exhilarating ride through the realm of personal transformation. His unique approach, captured in five distinct batteries, each charged with lessons and insights, offers a refreshing perspective on how to navigate the complexities of modern life.

The journey begins with Battery #1 – "FOCUS to Thrive," where David emphasizes the importance of setting clear intentions and mastering the art of prioritization. He shares his wisdom on how to break free from the constant hustle and embrace meaningful productivity. With every page, you'll be reminded that time is a finite treasure, and how you choose to spend it matters.

Battery #2 – "FREEDOM to Flourish" delves into the importance of breaking free from distractions and negative habits. David's personal anecdotes and reflections offer a guide to becoming the best version of oneself, filled with purpose and devoid of self-doubt.

Battery #3 – "FAITH to Fly" is a powerful testament to the significance of belief and self-confidence. As David takes us through the journey of nurturing our belief systems, you'll discover the limitless potential that resides within you.

Battery #4 – "FORCE to Succeed" resonates with those who understand that success requires not just hope but hard work. David emphasizes the law of motion and how embracing the heat can transform good into great.

Finally, Battery #5 – "FUN The Fuel of Fulfillment" is a reminder that amidst the striving and achieving, there's a vital place for joy and laughter. David invites you to embrace the art & science of fun and discover the fulfillment that it brings to life.

Throughout this book, David combines personal stories, practical advice, and deep reflection to offer a roadmap for those who seek to lead purpose-driven lives. With each battery, he guides you through the process of charging yourself up with the energy and mindset required to pursue your goals with fervor.

"Batteries not included" is a testament to the strength of the human spirit and the ability to transcend challenges. David's story is one of transformation and resilience, and his wisdom will undoubtedly inspire you to live your life charged with focus, faith, freedom, force, and fun.

As you embark on this transformative journey through the pages of this book, remember that just as David has evolved from DJ to world-changer, you too can power your purpose and be "All Charged Up."

So, grab this book, turn the page, and let David be your guide to a more charged-up and purpose-driven life. It is a journey well worth taking.

-Karl Phillips

INTRODUCTION

Tis' the Season for BATTERIES

The Christmas season has always held a special place in my heart. The air is filled with joy and cheer, and the spirit of generosity flows through the streets. I find myself captivated by the enchanting movies (Home Alone & Elf especially) that transport me to magical worlds and the melodies of timeless carols and Christmas pop songs that warm my soul - Christmas just ain't Christmas without Mariah Carey in the background. The festive decorations adorning every corner of the town create a picturesque scene, as if straight out of a storybook.

It's a time when I gather with my loved ones, creating treasured memories through delightful traditions. I cherish the moments spent with my children, driving through neighborhoods adorned with shimmering decorations, their eyes filled with wonder and excitement. We revel in the joy of exchanging presents, wrapping each gesture of love in colorful paper and bows. As we sip hot cocoa & make s'mores by the crackling fireplace, laughter fills the air, and the warmth of togetherness envelops us. Christmas reminds me of the immeasurable blessings of family and the joy that flourishes when we come together to celebrate the season of love and giving. I love Christmas so much, in 2022 I left my Christmas tree up in the living room for the entire year!!!

Amidst the twinkling lights and bustling holiday stores, there's one phrase that seems to echo louder than any other: *"batteries not included."* It became a familiar refrain when exchanging gifts, especially those containing electronics. It struck me how often the excitement of receiving a new gadget or toy was met with the realization that an additional power source was required for it to fulfill its purpose. Even the most thoughtfully chosen presents often needed an extra boost to truly come alive.

This observation, however, extended far beyond the realm of material objects. It served as a metaphor, a gentle nudge from within, urging me to delve deeper into the nature of our own gifts—the talents, hopes, purposes, and dreams that reside within each of us. Just like those electronic gifts, our own potential requires the right batteries, the essential tools, to be activated and powered.

Just like those electronic gifts, our own potential requires the right batteries, the essential tools, to be activated and powered. The ever elusive American Dream we were all sold as kids--the great career, perfect family, big house with 2.5 kids and a dog--the lavish life of the rich and famous, or the dream of becoming a professional athlete, or making it out of the hood.... Whatever dreams you were sold or gifts you were given, they all require the right batteries to come alive! And so, the inspiration for this book was born—a guide to help you discover and connect the right batteries or tools that will fuel your future, propelling you toward a purpose-driven life.

> Whatever dreams you were sold or gifts you were given, they all require the right batteries to come alive!

Welcome to **"Batteries Not Included: *How to Power Your Purpose & Fuel Your Future,"*** where we embark on a journey to identify and cultivate the sources of power that will energize your unique talents and aspirations. Throughout the chapters ahead, we will explore the fundamental principles and practical strategies that will empower you to unleash your full potential. Together, we will learn how to select and integrate the batteries—be it knowledge, skills, mindset, or relationships—that align perfectly with your individual gifts. Prepare to embark on a transformative quest, where you will gain the tools and insights necessary to illuminate your path and infuse your purpose with unwavering clarity and confidence. Let's get it!!

DISCLAIMER - WARNING!

Before we delve into the heart of the matter, it is crucial to set the record straight and establish the right expectations. The following five batteries we are about to explore—Freedom, Faith, Focus, Force, and Fun—are not intended to serve as an end-all, be-all solution or an exhaustive approach to fueling your future or powering your purpose. They represent powerful elements that have proven transformative in my personal journey, as well as in the lives of numerous influential and productive individuals I have had the privilege to work with and encounter throughout my career.

However, it is important to recognize that each person's path is unique, and what works for one may not necessarily work in the same way for another. These batteries are tools for you to consider and explore, drawing inspiration and insights from them as you navigate your own journey towards fulfillment and success.

Battery 1: The FOCUS to Thrive

In the first chapter, we dive into the power of Focus as a vital tool for achieving clarity and maximizing our potential. Focus encompasses the ability to direct our attention and energy towards our priorities, eliminating distractions and cultivating a disciplined mindset. We will explore techniques to sharpen our focus, enhance productivity, and stay present in the pursuit of our goals. Through practical exercises and mindfulness practices, we will navigate the path of focus, unlocking the transformative impact it has on our lives. Remember, focus is a skill that can be honed, and this chapter will equip you with the tools to cultivate laser-like focus and thrive in your endeavors.

> Focus encompasses the ability to direct our attention and energy towards our priorities, eliminating distractions and cultivating a disciplined mindset.

Battery 2: The FREEDOM to Flourish

In the second chapter, we explore the power of Freedom as a catalyst for unleashing our true potential. What are the things that we need to free ourselves from or cut or eliminate from our lives in order to flourish! Freedom encompasses breaking free from self-imposed limitations, societal expectations, and fear of judgment. We will delve into the importance of authenticity, self-expression, and living in alignment with our core values. Through inspiring stories and practical exercises, we will uncover ways to cultivate a sense of inner freedom, enabling us to make choices that align with our true selves. Remember, true freedom begins from within, and this chapter will empower you to embrace the liberation that comes with living authentically.

Battery 3: The FAITH to Fly

In the third chapter, we delve into the power of belief as the driving force behind our achievements. Belief is the cornerstone of self-confidence, resilience, and the realization of our aspirations. We'll explore practical techniques to nurture a strong belief system, conquer self-doubt, and embrace challenges with unwavering determination. Through inspiring stories and actionable strategies, we'll guide you on a transformative journey of self-discovery, harnessing the full potential of your beliefs to pursue your goals.

> Belief encompasses having faith in ourselves, our abilities, and the possibility of our dreams coming to fruition.

Battery 4: The FORCE to Succeed

In the fourth chapter we explore the power of force, the driving energy propelling us toward success. Force entails deliberate, consistent action, fueled by determination and a robust work ethic. We'll uncover strategies to conquer procrastination, cultivate discipline, and sustain momentum on your purpose-driven journey. Through real-life examples and practical techniques, we empower you to harness your inner drive and take intentional action, turning your dreams into tangible achievements. Remember, force is not pressure but a source of empowerment. This chapter will guide you to embrace the power of force and unlock your full potential.

Battery 5: FUN - The Fuel of Fulfillment

In this fifth and final chapter, we uncover the transformative power of fun as the driving force behind our fulfillment. Fun isn't just a pleasant diversion; it's a catalyst for creativity, innovation, and embracing joy in our journey. Through engaging stories and practical activities, we'll explore how infusing fun into our daily lives can lead to increased enthusiasm, resilience, and a brighter perspective. Remember, fun is not the opposite of success; it's an essential ingredient for achieving true fulfillment. This chapter will equip you to harness the energy of fun to unlock your potential and savor the path to your dreams.

With these F batteries (Focus, Freedom, Faith, Force, & Fun) as our fuel, let us embark on a transformative journey of self-discovery and purposeful living. Remember, your journey is unique, and these batteries are tools to ignite and inspire you along the way. As we explore each chapter, I encourage you to reflect, apply the principles, and adapt them to suit your individual needs and aspirations.

FOCUS
TO THRIVE

'Where your focus goes, your energy flows'
—Eric Thomas

DAVID SETTLE

READY, AIM, FIRE!

As we prepare to install these batteries that fuel our future and power our purpose, it is crucial to emphasize the importance of using our newfound gifts for their intended purpose. Much like installing batteries in a device, we need to ensure that our talents, skills, and aspirations are channeled & focused towards a clear, specific, and measurable target or goal. We must ask ourselves, 'What's the point!?'

Almost every instructional manual for any electronic device has a section that warns users that the device in question must be used for its intended purpose. And oftentimes if users fail to comply with the intended purpose, not only will the device fail to function properly and limit its productivity, but also voids certain warranties!

I don't care what it is… an Xbox 360 should not be used as a stepstool, smartphones aren't designed to be used as door stoppers, and laptops shouldn't be used as frisbees! Using any of these devices in these ways not only limits our ability to experience their benefits, but also could cause catastrophic complications!!

Just as electronic devices provide instructions to help users maximize performance and minimize malfunctions, understanding the importance of using our gifts and talents for their intended purpose is crucial. When we align our abilities with a clear goal or target, we unlock their full potential and make a meaningful impact. This principle applies

> When we align our abilities with a clear goal or target, we unlock their full potential and make a meaningful impact.

not only to devices but also to our personal growth and achievements. In simpler terms, it all comes down to one question: *What's the point?*

Speaking of using our gifts for their intended purposes, let me share a personal story that really brings this concept to life. Back in high school, I had this crazy knack for math. I mean, numbers just clicked with me, it was truly a gift, and I couldn't get enough of subjects like algebra, geometry, trigonometry, statistics, economics, and even calculous. Don't let my tattoos fool you, I was a bit of a math nerd deep down.

But here's where things got interesting. Instead of using my mathematical prowess to ace my classes and pursue a career in a field like business, finance, or even engineering (yeah, I know, rocket science was a bit of a stretch), I ended up taking a different path. I got caught up in the wrong crowd and started using my math skills for, uh, let's say less-than-legal activities. Yep, I became a bit of a math-savvy drug dealer, figuring out ways to make a profit by doing calculations, converting units of measure and breaking down large quantities for local distribution in order to scale my operations. I was good at it, no doubt about that. But man, I was using my gifts in all the wrong ways. Similar to one using their laptop as a frisbee!

Luckily, life had a way of giving me a wake-up call. I realized I was on a dangerous path and decided to make a major shift in my life. I discovered my true calling and passion for legitimate business ventures. It was like a lightbulb moment, you know? I started using my math skills for their intended purpose, aligned with my newfound aspirations.

So, the lesson here is this: we all have unique gifts and talents, and it's up to us to use them wisely. We've got to find our true purpose and channel our abilities towards something positive and meaningful. When we do that, we unleash our full potential and make a real impact on the world. It's a journey, my friend, but one worth taking.

> We all have unique gifts and talents, and it's up to us to use them wisely.

By defining our target or goal, we give our purpose a tangible form. We give ourselves a target to aim at and a goal to strive for. Our goals serve as a beacon that draws us forward, igniting a sense of determination and resilience within us. This target serves as a constant reminder of what we strive to achieve, driving us to take the necessary steps and make the right choices aligned with our purpose.

Moreover, a specific and measurable target allows us to track our progress and evaluate our actions. Just as a battery's energy can be measured by the power it provides, our efforts and actions can be assessed against the milestones we set. This evaluation helps us adjust our course, celebrate our successes, and learn from any setbacks we encounter along the way.

Remember, without a clear target to aim at or a specific goal to reach for, installing the batteries of purpose is futile, rendering our efforts and potential meaningless. It is the clear and specific target or goal that gives our purpose direction and amplifies our impact. So, let us set our sights on a meaningful destination, ensuring that our newfound gifts are utilized purposefully, and our actions align with our aspirations. With a clear target in mind, we can activate our purpose, harness our potential, and embark on a journey of growth, fulfillment, and accomplishment.

I recall a time my son and I nearly starved to death because we lacked a specific target or destination! Allow me to explain.... One day when my son and I set out to find a place to eat we found ourselves without a specific restaurant in mind, so we decided to embark on an adventure, hoping that something would catch our attention along the way.

With excitement and hunger driving us, we hopped into the car and started driving aimlessly, exploring different streets and neighborhoods. As time passed, our hunger grew, but we remained determined to stumble upon a place that piqued our interest. Little did we realize that our lack of a clear destination or target would lead us on an unintended journey of frustration.

As the minutes eclipsed an hour, our aimless driving began to take its toll. We found ourselves driving in circles, going down unfamiliar roads and retracing our steps. With each passing moment, our hunger intensified, and our frustration mounted. The lack of direction became evident as we wasted precious time, gas, and energy in our quest for a simple meal.

The once-exciting adventure had turned into a disheartening experience. Our growling stomachs served as a constant reminder of our misguided approach. It was evident that without a clear destination, we were merely spinning our wheels and exacerbating our frustrations.

Finally, realizing the futility of our aimless endeavor, we decided to regroup. We pulled over, took a moment to reflect, and searched for nearby restaurants. Within minutes, we had a clear destination in mind—Whataburger - God's gift to Texas!

The relief was near as we navigated towards the restaurant with purpose. Our hunger was finally satisfied, and our frustrations began to dissipate. The experience taught us a valuable lesson about the importance of having a clear destination or target. In this simple journey, we witnessed firsthand how the absence of a clear goal resulted in wasted time, energy, and resources. It highlighted the significance of setting a specific destination, whether in our daily lives or on grander endeavors. Just as in our search for a place to eat, having a clear goal guides our actions, optimizes our efforts, and ensures a more fulfilling and rewarding outcome.

From that day forward, we embarked on our adventures with a renewed sense of purpose, ensuring that we always had a clear destination in mind. The experience served as a powerful reminder to approach life's journeys with clarity, intention, and a specific target, allowing us to make the most of our time, energy, and appetite for life's experiences.

Success in various domains relies on the establishment of specific targets and setting clear goals. Basketball players aim for the hoop, relying on a precise target to guide their shots and determine their scoring. Pilots set their sights on specific destinations, ensuring a safe and purposeful flight. In the realm of photography, capturing the perfect shot often requires a specific target or subject, as it provides a focal point and enhances the overall composition. These examples underscore the significance of having

BATTERIES NOT INCLUDED

clear targets in different fields, as they provide direction, focus efforts, and increase the chances of achieving desired outcomes.

Without targets, we risk wandering aimlessly, wasting valuable resources and diluting our potential for success. By setting specific goals and targets, we create a roadmap that propels us forward, allowing us to measure progress, make intentional choices, and channel our energy effectively. So, let us embrace the power of specificity, chart our course with purpose, and unlock our true potential by setting clear goals and targets that light our path to achievement and fulfillment.

> Without targets, we risk wandering aimlessly, wasting valuable resources and diluting our potential for success.

JACK OF ALL TRADES, MASTER OF NONE

I want to drive this point home a little further, because there is an element of focus that goes beyond simply setting targets and establishing goals. Once the goal has been set, we can now focus our energy and effort on that particular target enhancing our efficiency, powering our productivity, and strengthening our efforts! The best way I can explain this phenomenon is by observing a lumberjack wielding his ax at the same point over and over and over again until the tree comes down!

I want you to imagine a lumberjack in action. Picture them swinging their ax with precision, aiming at the exact same spot on the tree trunk repeatedly. Each swing is deliberate, focused, and calculated. They don't waste their energy by striking the tree randomly or haphazardly. Instead, they concentrate all their strength and effort on that one specific target. Over, and over, and over, and over! With every powerful swing, they inch closer to bringing down the tree.

Now, consider what would happen if the lumberjack swung their ax randomly, striking the tree at multiple spots without a clear focus. The energy and effort would be dispersed, resulting in a scattered impact. It would take much longer, if ever, for the tree to fall. The lack of concentration and direction would diminish their effectiveness and prolong the task at hand.

The same principle applies to us as individuals. When we have a specific goal or target in mind, directing our energy and efforts toward it becomes paramount. By focusing our attention, concentration, and resources on that particular objective, we enhance our efficiency and effectiveness. We tap into our full potential and channel our efforts in a way that yields greater results.

> By focusing our attention, concentration, and resources on that particular objective, we enhance our efficiency and effectiveness.

Without a clear focus, our energy becomes dispersed, our productivity suffers, and our progress may be hindered. But when we fix our sights on a specific goal, we harness the power of focus to drive us forward. We become more intentional, purposeful, and directed in our actions. It is through this unwavering focus that we can achieve remarkable feats and unlock our true potential.

So, let us swing for success just like a lumberjack swings their ax, channeling our energy, strength, and determination toward the specific target we have set. By focusing our efforts, we can maximize our productivity, overcome obstacles, and accomplish what once seemed insurmountable. With a clear focus and unwavering determination, we can power our purpose and bring our goals within reach.

I've shared this theory with so many entrepreneurs and professionals over the years, especially those who struggle with being a jack of all trades and master of none! In our modern world, there is a pervasive notion that we need to be proficient in multiple areas, wearing numerous hats and juggling countless responsibilities. We are often told that versatility is the key to success, but what often gets overlooked is the power of specialization and focused expertise.

And I have to admit that I, too, have found myself facing this challenge head-on. As I reflect on my own journey, I realize that I've worn many hats and pursued various endeavors, striving to excel in each one. I've been a DJ, an educator, a family man, a minister, an author, a photographer, an entrepreneur, and the list goes on. While I was proficient in these roles, the true test was whether I could achieve greatness in any one of them.

It became clear that my energy was being divided, my focus diluted, and my efforts scattered across multiple pursuits. It was time for me to take a hard look in the mirror and confront the reality that being a jack of all trades was hindering my ability to truly master any. The importance of focus and specialization began to resonate deeply within me.

DAVID SETTLE

During the early years of my first business, DJS Entertainment, a prominent wedding entertainment firm in Houston, I would eagerly accept any DJ gig that came my way. Birthdays, weddings, corporate events, sweet 16s, bar mitzvahs, festivals—you name it, I DJ'd it all. However, I soon realized that spreading myself too thin was preventing me from truly excelling in any particular area.

One day, a pivotal decision changed the trajectory of my business. I made the conscious choice to narrow my focus and concentrate all my energy, marketing efforts, and resources on attracting weddings and newly engaged couples. I committed wholeheartedly to becoming the best wedding DJ and emcee in the city. It was a strategic shift that paid off tremendously.

By specializing in the wedding industry, my humble side-hustle experienced a remarkable transformation. Annual revenues skyrocketed from a modest $30,000 to over $250,000 in a short period of time. I went from working alone to having a team of talented professionals supporting me. The power of focusing my efforts and specializing in one area became abundantly clear.

This personal experience serves as a testament to the incredible impact that can be achieved when we concentrate our energy and resources on a specific goal. It highlights the importance of specializing and becoming exceptional in a chosen field rather than being merely good in multiple areas. By narrowing our focus, we unlock the potential for exponential growth and success.

When we try to be a jack of all trades, we may find ourselves spreading our energy and efforts thin. We become generalists, tackling a wide array of tasks without delving deeply into any one area. While this approach may initially seem appealing or even necessary, it can lead to a lack of true mastery and hinder our progress. We may become competent in various domains, but without specialization, our impact and effectiveness may be limited. We are left with only amounting to being 'good' instead of 'great.'

By focusing our energy and efforts on a specific target or area of expertise, we can unlock a higher level of mastery. Just as the lumberjack concentrates their swings on a single spot of the tree trunk, we can direct our attention, resources, and time toward honing our skills and deepening our knowledge in a particular field. This level of specialization allows us to develop a deeper understanding, refine our abilities, and achieve a level of proficiency that sets us apart.

> By focusing our energy and efforts on a specific target or area of expertise, we can unlock a higher level of mastery.

Specialization doesn't mean disregarding other areas entirely. It means prioritizing and dedicating significant time and effort to a core focus while still maintaining a broad awareness of related disciplines. This deliberate narrowing of focus empowers us to delve deeper into our chosen field, staying up-to-date with emerging trends, technologies, and advancements. It enables us to offer unique value, become sought-after experts, and make a lasting impact in our respective industries.

In a world where information is readily available and distractions abound, it is easy to fall into the trap of trying to do it all. However, by embracing the power of specialization, we can rise above the noise and stand out from the crowd. We can leverage our expertise to solve complex problems, innovate, and make meaningful contributions. It is through this focused approach that we can truly excel, transforming from a jack of all trades into a master of our chosen craft.

> By embracing the power of specialization, we can rise above the noise and stand out from the crowd.

So, let us remember that being a master of one trade does not diminish our versatility or potential. Rather, it amplifies our impact, deepens our understanding, and allows us to achieve greatness in a specific domain. Embrace the power of focus and specialization, set your sights on a specific target, and watch as your expertise grows, your influence expands, and your purpose becomes even more powerful.

Now, I invite you to take a moment and evaluate your current goals or set new ones. As you embark on this transformative journey, it is essential to have a clear destination in mind. Without goals, the following pages may feel purposeless, like wandering without a compass. So, grab a pen, perhaps some coffee and physically write down your goals or something you aspire to achieve as a result of working through this book. Let these words on the page serve as a commitment, a declaration of your intent to unlock your true potential and power your purpose. With your goals in hand, you hold the key to steering your life towards meaningful accomplishments. Embrace this opportunity and let your goals be the driving force that propels you forward on this extraordinary path of self-discovery and growth.

REFLECTIONS/TAKEAWAYS

Remember, self-reflection is a powerful tool for gaining clarity and setting meaningful goals. Take the time to delve into these questions, write down your thoughts, and use them as a foundation for defining your goals and crafting a purposeful path forward.

What truly matters to you?

> Take a moment to identify the aspects of your life that hold deep significance and bring you joy. Consider your values, passions, and the activities that make you feel fulfilled. Reflect on what truly matters to you and align your goals with those core values.

Where do you see yourself in the future?

> Envision the future version of yourself, whether it's in one year, five years, or even ten years from now. What does your ideal life look like? What accomplishments have you achieved? Use this vision as a guide to set goals that will bring you closer to that desired future

What specific area of your life would you like to improve or make significant progress in?

> Take a moment to reflect on the different aspects of your life, such as career, relationships, health, personal development, or any other area that holds importance to you. Identify one specific area where you feel a strong desire for growth or change. This could be a skill you want to develop, a project you want to complete, a milestone you want to reach, or a habit you want to cultivate. By pinpointing a specific area, you can set a clear target or goal that will guide your actions and measure your progress.

Remember, specificity is key when setting goals. By focusing on a particular area for improvement or growth, you can channel your efforts and resources more effectively, increasing your chances of success. Use this question as a starting point to identify the specific target or goal that will inspire and motivate you throughout your journey of personal and professional development

FREEDOM
TO FLOURISH

"Your net worth to the world is usually determined by what remains after your bad habits are subtracted from your good ones."
—Benjamin Franklin

"The Soul does not grow by addition but by subtraction."
—Meister Eckhart

Subtraction has a bad rep! Typically when we refer to subtraction, it's with a negative (no pun intended) connotation! We use synonyms like 'negative,' 'loss,' 'eliminate,' or 'deficit.' However, subtraction can be one of our most powerful allies in reaching our goals! By strategically subtracting the nonessential, the distractions, and the energy-draining elements from our lives, we create space and clarity to focus on what truly matters. Subtraction becomes a catalyst for transformation and a pathway to success.

> By strategically subtracting the nonessential, the distractions, and the energy-draining elements from our lives, we create space and clarity to focus on what truly matters.

In a world that often celebrates accumulation and addition, we tend to overlook the incredible power of subtraction. We are conditioned to believe that more is always better, that success is measured by how much we can accumulate or acquire. But what if we shifted our perspective? What if we recognized that sometimes, the key to progress lies in letting go, in shedding the unnecessary, and in simplifying?

Subtraction allows us to streamline our efforts, hone our focus, and direct our energy towards what truly aligns with our goals and values. It empowers us to make intentional choices and prioritize the essential. Just like an artist chisels away at a block of marble to reveal a masterpiece, we

> Subtraction allows us to streamline our efforts, hone our focus, and direct our energy towards what truly aligns with our goals and values.

BATTERIES NOT INCLUDED

too can chisel away the excess in our lives to uncover our true potential and purpose.

We will explore how letting go of and being set free from what no longer serves us can create space for growth, innovation, and fulfillment. Through practical strategies, insightful anecdotes, and reflective exercises, we will uncover the art of purposeful subtraction, allowing us to recharge our lives, ignite our passions, and pursue our goals with unwavering focus and clarity.

So, let us embrace the often-underestimated power of subtraction and embark on a journey that liberates us from the burdens of excess. Together, we will discover that by subtracting the unnecessary, we unlock the extraordinary and create a life that is truly aligned with our deepest aspirations.

FREE FROM DISTRACTIONS

In order to increase focus and productivity, it's essential to decrease distractions. This could involve limiting time spent on social media, turning off notifications, or creating a dedicated work environment free from interruptions.

> In order to increase focus and productivity, it's essential to decrease distractions.

You know, my eyesight has been a challenge for me practically my whole life. I've had to wear glasses just to see clearly. Without them, everything around me turns into a blurry mess. It's pretty hilarious actually, even those eye charts they make you read at the optometrist's office... I can barely make out the biggest letters at the very top! I'm practically blind without my trusty glasses (or contacts) saving my sight! And one of the most annoying things about wearing glasses is having a smudge or any impairment on the lense!!

Imagine wearing a pair of glasses with smudges and fingerprints all over the lenses. Despite your best efforts, everything you look at appears hazy and unclear. To truly see with clarity, you instinctively reach for a cleaning cloth and wipe away the distractions that hinder your vision. In the same way, removing distractions from our lives is like cleaning our mental lenses, allowing us to gain a clear perspective and focus on our purpose.

Just as smudges on glasses distort our view, distractions cloud our minds and divert our attention away from what truly matters. Social media notifications, constant email alerts, and interruptions disrupt our flow of thoughts, preventing us from delving deep into our work. By consciously limiting our time spent on social media, turning off notifications, and creating a distraction-free work environment, we embark on a journey of cleansing our mental lenses.

As we remove the smudges of distractions, our vision becomes clearer, enabling us to see our goals and purpose with renewed focus. Like a photographer adjusting the focus on a camera lens, we fine-tune our mental clarity, ensuring that our attention is directed towards what truly deserves it. We become more present and engaged, able to immerse ourselves fully in the task at hand, and make significant strides towards our objectives.

By cleaning our mental lenses and removing distractions, we create a space for clarity and purpose to thrive. Just as the act of cleaning glasses allows us to see the world in all its vivid details, eliminating distractions opens up a world of possibilities, where we can fully embrace our true potential and accomplish our goals with greater precision and effectiveness. So, let us take the necessary steps to wipe away the smudges of distractions and see our path forward with unparalleled clarity

Distractions of all sorts have become an ever-present challenge in our modern lives, hindering our ability to focus and be productive. In a world filled with constant notifications, buzzing smartphones, and endless streams of information, our attention is constantly pulled in different directions. The negative effects of distractions are far-reaching, impacting our work, relationships, and overall well-being.

When we allow distractions to take hold, our focus becomes fragmented, leading to decreased productivity and efficiency. We find ourselves multitasking, jumping from one task to another without fully engaging or completing any of them. This not only diminishes the quality of our work but also prolongs the time it takes to accomplish our goals. Distractions disrupt our thought processes, making it difficult to concentrate and think deeply, stifling creativity and innovation in the process.

Moreover, distractions can negatively impact our emotional well-being. Constant exposure to social media feeds, news updates, or comparison traps can lead to feelings of inadequacy, anxiety, and a sense of being overwhelmed. Our ability to be fully present and engaged in our personal relationships suffers as well, as our attention is diverted away from those who matter most.

I've often referred to this phenomenon as having limited mental bandwidth, similar to any finite resource that we must allocate wisely. Just like a computer processor with a limited capacity, our minds can only handle a certain amount of information and tasks at any given time. When we allow distractions to overload our mental bandwidth, our productivity and effectiveness suffer, as we struggle to process and prioritize the influx of stimuli vying for our attention.

This makes me think about the little spinning wheel of death on my macbook. Y'all know exactly what I'm talking about.... We've all seen it (well those of us smart enough to have Macbooks lol). Some refer to it as the beachball of death, but it's the animated rainbow spinning wheel that lets users know something is loading. It typically appears when the system or a specific application is experiencing a significant delay or unresponsiveness. The spinning wheel is an indicator that the Macbook is struggling to process the tasks or data it is being asked to handle, often due to high system resource usage, insufficient memory, or a complex operation. It signifies that the system is temporarily overloaded and unable to perform tasks smoothly, prompting the user to wait until it regains stability.

Just like the spinning wheel on a Macbook signifies system overload, our minds can also become overwhelmed and overloaded by distractions, impeding our focus and productivity. In the digital age, we face a constant barrage of notifications, information, and demands for our attention. This influx of stimuli can easily push our mental capacities to their limits, much like the spinning wheel symbolizes an overwhelmed system.

When we allow distractions to take hold, our mental state mimics the spinning wheel's unresponsiveness. Our thoughts become fragmented, our ability to concentrate falters, and our productivity suffers. We find ourselves trapped in a cycle of shifting focus between various tasks, unable to fully engage with any one of them. Just as the spinning wheel slows down a Macbook's performance, distractions bog down our mental processes, hindering our ability to make progress and achieve optimal results.

However, by recognizing the parallels between the spinning wheel of death and our mental state, we can take proactive steps to regain control. We must consciously reduce distractions, establish boundaries, and cultivate a focused environment. This intentional effort allows us to free up mental resources, similar to resolving the spinning wheel issue, and restore our mental capacity for deeper concentration and productive work.

In essence, by managing distractions and avoiding mental overload, we can prevent our minds from entering a state akin to the spinning wheel of a Macbook. We can reclaim our mental clarity, unlock our true potential, and operate at our most efficient and effective levels. Just as slowing down and shutting down certain applications and processes resolves the spinning wheel issue and restores a Macbook's responsiveness, taking control of our mental state by freeing ourselves from distractions allows us to navigate tasks with clarity and purpose, achieving meaningful results.

Imagine trying to juggle multiple tasks while bombarded with constant notifications, interruptions, and distractions. Each additional demand on our mental bandwidth diminishes our ability to focus and make progress. Our thoughts become scattered, our decision-making falters, and our productivity dwindles. It's essential to recognize that the quality of our work and our ability to achieve meaningful outcomes are directly impacted by how effectively we manage and allocate our mental bandwidth.

By consciously minimizing distractions, creating boundaries, and cultivating a focused work environment, we can optimize our mental bandwidth. This intentional approach allows us to allocate our cognitive resources to the tasks that truly matter, leading to enhanced concentration, deeper engagement, and ultimately, heightened productivity. It's through this intentional preservation and allocation of our mental bandwidth that we can unlock our true potential and accomplish our goals with greater efficiency and effectiveness.

However, by consciously removing distractions from our lives, we unlock a multitude of positive ramifications. When we limit time spent on social media, we regain control over our attention and redirect it toward more meaningful pursuits. Turning off notifications allows us to reclaim our focus, enabling us to delve deeper into our work or personal projects. Creating a dedicated work environment free from interruptions cultivates an atmosphere conducive to concentration and creativity.

> By consciously removing distractions from our lives, we unlock a multitude of positive ramifications.

BATTERIES NOT INCLUDED

As distractions are diminished, we experience heightened focus and increased productivity. Our work becomes more efficient and of higher quality as we can give our full attention to the task at hand. By being fully present and engaged in our interactions, we nurture stronger connections and deeper relationships. Removing distractions also allows us to tap into our inner creativity, unlocking new ideas and fresh perspectives.

> As distractions are diminished, we experience heightened focus and increased productivity.

Furthermore, the positive ramifications of removing distractions extend beyond immediate outcomes. We reclaim valuable time and energy that can be redirected towards activities aligned with our goals and values. We gain a sense of clarity and purpose, knowing that we are intentionally choosing how to invest our time and attention. Ultimately, by removing distractions, we empower ourselves to live more intentionally and fully engage in the moments that truly matter.

By prioritizing what truly matters and creating intentional boundaries, you will discover the transformative effects of removing distractions and paving the way for powering your purpose and fueling your future!

REFLECTIONS/TAKEAWAYS

As you embark on the journey of self-reflection and self-evaluation, it's important to recognize that the examples of external distractions we discussed earlier and the list below are by no means exhaustive. They merely represent just a few examples of the common distractions that can hinder our focus and productivity.

However, the purpose of this exercise is not to create an exhaustive inventory but rather to ignite your awareness and prompt you to reflect on the distractions that may be prevalent in your own life. With this understanding, I encourage you to take a closer look at the list and consider the distractions that resonate with you the most. Highlight or circle those that have a significant impact on your ability to stay focused and on track. Remember, this is a personalized journey, and your unique set of distractions may differ from others. By focusing on your own experiences, you can gain valuable insights into areas where you can make positive changes.

- *Social media notifications*
- *Email and instant message alerts*
- *Television and streaming services*
- *Noisy neighbors or outside noise*
- *Phone calls and text messages*
- *Cluttered or disorganized work environment*
- *Co-workers or colleagues interrupting*
- *Meetings and unnecessary work-related events*
- *News and media updates*
- *Constant barrage of advertisements*

- *Traffic or noisy commute*
- *Family or household responsibilities*
- *Unexpected visitors or social obligations*
- *Gaming or video game distractions*
- *Office politics and gossip*
- *Excessive multitasking*
- *Online shopping or browsing*
- *Uncomfortable or distracting physical environment*
- *Procrastination-inducing activities*
- *Poorly structured or inefficient work processes*

To further deepen your reflection, I invite you to engage with the following questions as you explore the impact of these distractions and contemplate potential solutions:

Beyond the distractions listed, what other external factors tend to divert my attention and hinder my productivity?

....
....
....

How do these distractions align with my long-term goals and purpose? In what ways do they detract from my progress?

....
....
....

What strategies or practices can I implement to minimize or manage these distractions effectively?

....
....
....

By acknowledging that this list is just a starting point and embracing the broader scope of distractions in your life, you open yourself up to a more comprehensive evaluation. This will enable you to craft targeted solutions and develop a personalized approach to reducing distractions, reclaiming your focus, and empowering your purpose.

By honestly assessing the distractions that affect you the most and identifying the steps you can take to address them, you empower yourself to create a more conducive environment for achieving your goals. Use these reflections as an opportunity to prioritize your time, establish boundaries, and cultivate a greater sense of focus and productivity. Remember, the power to minimize external distractions and get FOCUSED lies within you.

FREE FROM NEGATIVE HABITS

Here's where the hard work comes into play! Because we can't begin to talk about bad habits, without being completely honest with ourselves, as we self evaluate the things that we do on a regular basis, especially when no one is watching!

So before we embark on this journey of self discovery, let's attempt to differentiate habits and distractions.

The simplest way I know how to describe the differences is that distractions tend to be external hindrances exerted upon someone, whereas bad habits are internally ingrained patterns of behavior that come from within.

Let's break it down further...

Bad habits are repetitive behaviors that hinder one's well-being, productivity, and success, while distractions divert our attention from our intended tasks or goals. Bad habits, such as procrastination or overspending, are detrimental patterns that can impede progress in our pursuit of purpose and fulfillment.

On the other hand, distractions, whether they originate externally or internally, have the potential to disrupt our focus and reduce our productivity. While some distractions may be temporary and spontaneous, bad habits are deeply ingrained patterns that require conscious effort to overcome. It is important to recognize both the influence of bad habits and the impact of distractions as we seek to empower our purpose and fuel our future

Now that we have a clear understanding of the distinction between habits and distractions we can move on to uprooting the bad habits in our lives that hinder positive habits from being fruitful. To cultivate positive habits, negative ones must be decreased or eliminated. This could involve cutting back on unhealthy eating habits, reducing procrastination, or breaking free from self-limiting beliefs.

In order to truly power our purpose, it is crucial to liberate ourselves from negative habits that hold us back and hinder our growth. These negative habits, whether they are related to our physical, mental, or emotional well-being, have the power to undermine our progress and prevent us from reaching our full potential. By consciously freeing ourselves from these detrimental patterns, we create space for positive habits to flourish and propel us towards success.

> By consciously freeing ourselves from these detrimental patterns, we create space for positive habits to flourish and propel us towards success.

Replacing negative habits with positive ones is a powerful way to shed light on our self-defeating patterns. As we discussed in the first chapter, where our focus goes, our energy follows. When we constantly fixate on avoiding negative behaviors, we inadvertently give them our attention, energy, and focus, leading to their persistence. However, by redirecting our focus towards positive alternatives, we can expect far more rewarding outcomes.

Numerous studies in psychology support the effectiveness of this approach. Research has shown that focusing on positive behaviors and goals is more productive and sustainable than solely trying to eliminate negative habits. By shifting our attention and energy towards constructive actions, we activate the motivational and reward systems in our brain, reinforcing positive habits and diminishing the hold of negative ones. This evidence-based approach not only helps us break free from detrimental patterns but also empowers us to cultivate lasting positive change in our lives.

In recent years, research in habit formation has provided a more nuanced understanding of the process. A study published in the European Journal of Social Psychology in 2009 examined the time it takes to form a habit and found that it ranged from 18 to 254 days, depending on the complexity of the behavior and individual differences.

This theory highlights the importance of recognizing that adopting positive behaviors requires time, patience, and **consistent** effort. It is unrealistic to expect immediate results or overnight transformations by simply making a decision or choice to change. True change necessitates **daily** commitment, discipline, determination, and perseverance, and most of all... **consistency**!

Countless studies on habit formation corroborate this perspective, suggesting that it takes an average of about three weeks for a behavior to become ingrained and automatic. During this period, consistent practice and repetition are essential to solidify the new habit and **override** old patterns. Patience and persistence are crucial as we navigate the challenges and setbacks that may arise along the way. By understanding the time and effort required to establish positive habits, we can approach the process with realistic expectations and maintain the motivation needed to stay the course. Remember, lasting change is a journey that unfolds **gradually**, but with consistent daily effort, the rewards will be well worth it in the end.

While there are countless habits that can impede progress and hinder individuals from reaching their goals, it is important to shed light on a few commonly encountered negative habits. These include procrastination, self-doubt, negative self-talk, perfectionism, and lack of discipline. However, it is crucial to acknowledge that no single book can encompass every single negative habit that exists. Furthermore, what might be a negative habit for one person may not necessarily be negative to another. The focus here is to emphasize the concept of replacing negative habits with positive ones and shifting our focus towards the positive aspects of our lives. By doing so, individuals can create a solid foundation for personal growth and propel themselves towards their desired outcomes.

In essence, the best way to get rid of something negative is to replace it with something positive!

In essence, the best way to get rid of something negative is to replace it with something positive!

One well-known figure with a story of replacing a bad habit with a good one is Robert Downey Jr. The actor struggled with addiction issues for many years but managed to turn his life around by replacing his destructive habits with positive ones.

Robert Downey Jr. had a long history of substance abuse and legal troubles in the 1990s and early 2000s. However, he decided to seek help and entered rehabilitation programs to overcome his addiction to drugs and alcohol. This marked the beginning of his journey toward recovery and personal transformation.

In his quest for a healthier and more fulfilling life, Downey Jr. replaced his old habits of substance abuse with new habits like regular exercise, meditation, and therapy. He also immersed himself in his work, focusing on his acting career with renewed dedication.

His perseverance paid off, and he made a remarkable comeback in Hollywood. He became one of the most iconic actors of his generation, best known for his role as Iron Man in the Marvel Cinematic Universe. Downey Jr. not only conquered his addiction but also became an inspiration for others facing similar challenges.

His story serves as a powerful example of how someone can replace destructive habits with positive ones and achieve personal and professional success, even after facing significant setbacks in life.

REFLECTIONS/TAKEAWAYS

In this chapter, we've delved into the importance of recognizing and replacing negative habits with positive ones to fuel our personal growth and journey towards purpose. Now, let's take a moment for self-reflection and practical action steps.

Identify Your Negative Habits:

Take a moment to reflect on your daily routines and behaviors, especially those you perform almost unconsciously or habitually.

Below, you'll find a list of 20 common negative habits in society. Circle or highlight those that resonate with you, the ones you'd like to eliminate or replace in your life.

Negative Habits:

- *Procrastination*
- *Self-doubt*
- *Negative self-talk*
- *Perfectionism*
- *Lack of discipline*
- *Overeating*
- *Excessive screen time*
- *Complaining*
- *Excessive spending*
- *Nail-biting*
- *Smoking*
- *Excessive alcohol consumption*
- *Skipping workouts*
- *Being chronically late*
- *Gossiping*
- *Dwelling on the past*
- *Clutter and disorganization*
- *Neglecting self-care*
- *Blaming others*
- *Ignoring financial responsibilities*

Replace with Positive Habits:

Now, *let's shift our focus to the positive. Below, you'll find a list of 20 positive behaviors and habits that can replace the negative ones you've circled or highlighted.*

Positive Habits:

- *Setting clear goals*
- *Practicing self-compassion*
- *Positive affirmations*
- *Setting realistic expectations*
- *Prioritizing self-care*
- *Mindfulness meditation*
- *Regular exercise*
- *Time management techniques*
- *Saving and budgeting*
- *Healthy eating habits*
- *Journaling for self-reflection*
- *Limiting screen time*
- *Acts of kindness*
- *Learning new skills*
- *Effective communication*
- *Cultivating gratitude*
- *Planning and organization*
- *Seeking support from a mentor or coach*
- *Setting boundaries*
- *Practicing patience*

Action Steps:

- [ ] Select at least one negative habit you've circled or highlighted.
- [ ] Identify the corresponding positive habit from the list above that you'd like to replace it with.
- [ ] Create a plan or strategy for incorporating positive habits into your daily routine.
- [ ] Start small and remain consistent in your efforts.
- [ ] Monitor your progress and make adjustments as needed.

Remember, the journey to replacing negative habits with positive ones is a gradual process that requires patience and persistence. Just as Robert Downey Jr. transformed his life by replacing destructive habits, you too can make meaningful changes that lead to personal growth, purpose, and fulfillment. Embrace this opportunity for self-improvement and watch as your positive habits propel you toward the life you desire.

FREEDOM FROM *DOIN' THE MOST* - PRIORITIZING PURPOSEFUL PRODUCTIVITY

In the relentless pace of our modern world, it's alarmingly easy to fall into the *doin' the most* trap—a perpetual state of busyness that masquerades as productivity. This chapter delves into the critical necessity of liberating ourselves from the shackles of excessive busyness and the profound impact prioritizing purpose-aligned tasks can have on our efficiency and overall contentment.

A PARALLEL TO FINANCIAL WISDOM

Managing time effectively, just like handling finances shrewdly, is a vital skill that lets us seize control of our precious resources. It's all about intention—just as you tell your money where to go to meet your financial goals, it's equally important to direct your time with purpose. As the old saying goes, 'manage your time or it will manage you!' Every minute is a new chance to make a meaningful mark, and being deliberate about where those minutes go is what separates those who dream from those who achieve.

For example, consider a writer with a full-time job who has a personal goal of completing a novel. Prioritizing novel writing means dedicating a set amount of time each day to work on it, even if it means sacrificing other less important activities. Just as you wouldn't spend your entire paycheck on frivolous purchases, you shouldn't squander your precious

> Prioritization helps you direct your time and energy toward activities that matter most, resulting in more significant accomplishments and personal fulfillment.

time on activities that don't contribute to your personal or professional growth. Prioritization helps you direct your time and energy toward activities that matter most, resulting in more significant accomplishments and personal fulfillment.

TIME: A FINITE TREASURE

Time is a finite and irreplaceable resource. Similar to how you manage your finances by ensuring that your expenses do not exceed your income, managing your time effectively involves making sure you allocate your hours wisely. Imagine your time as a treasure chest, and each task or activity you engage in as a coin from that chest. This perspective underscores the need to prioritize and invest your time wisely.

> Time is a finite and irreplaceable resource.

We are all given the same 24 hours in a day, and once they're gone, they're gone forever. Unlike an endless buffet, time is a finite, irreplaceable resource, more akin to a fine delicacy. Each hour should be savored like a rare and exquisite dish, chosen with intention to enrich our lives. As a discerning chef carefully selects ingredients to create a memorable meal, we too should be selective with our commitments, focusing on enriching experiences that add depth to our existence. Treating our time with such regard transforms it into a gourmet experience, filled with moments that are both fulfilling and memorable, crafting a life that truly satisfies.

THE ART OF PRIORITIZATION

> Delegation is like outsourcing the management of a portion of your time portfolio.

Prioritization is the cornerstone of both financial budgeting and time management. Just as in finances, you might enlist the help of financial advisors or automated investment tools to optimize your portfolio, in time management, you can delegate tasks that others can perform as efficiently or even better than you. Delegation is like outsourcing the management of a portion of your time portfolio.

For instance, if you're a business owner, you might delegate administrative tasks to an assistant or use automation tools for routine data entry. By doing so, you free up your time to focus on strategic decisions and business growth. In the world of personal finance, this is akin to entrusting a financial advisor to handle your investments while you concentrate on your career. Both in finances and time management, delegation and automation are powerful tools that allow you to leverage the expertise of others or the efficiency of technology to maximize your resources effectively.

INVESTING IN MEANING

In the realm of personal finance, wise individuals recognize the importance of investing in assets that appreciate over time or experiences that enrich their lives.

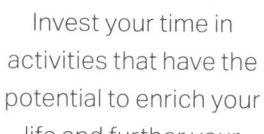

> Invest your time in activities that have the potential to enrich your life and further your personal or professional development.

Similarly, in the context of time management, we should adopt a similar mindset by investing our precious hours in tasks that yield meaning, personal growth, and satisfaction. Think of your time as a valuable stock portfolio. Just as you aim to invest in stocks with strong potential for growth, you should invest your time in activities that have the potential to enrich your life and further your personal or professional development.

Consider a scenario where you have a choice to spend your evening attending a networking event that aligns with your career goals or watching random videos on the internet. The networking event may not provide immediate gratification, but it has the potential to open doors to new opportunities and connections in the future. On the other hand, spending hours aimlessly surfing the web may be momentarily enjoyable but offers little long-term benefit. By choosing to invest your time in the networking event, you're making a deliberate choice to prioritize meaning and potential growth over fleeting entertainment.

THE MIRAGE OF CONSTANT ACTIVITY

In today's fast-paced world, it's all too common to fall into the trap of constant activity, believing that staying busy equates to being productive. This mirage can be likened to a treadmill. You're constantly moving, but you're not making any meaningful progress. You may start your day with a lengthy to-do list, tackling one task after another, yet by day's end, you may feel drained and wonder what you've truly accomplished.

Imagine you're at work, juggling multiple projects simultaneously. You answer emails, attend meetings, and engage in various tasks throughout the day. By evening, you're exhausted, yet when you reflect on your day, you realize that you haven't made significant progress on any of your key projects. This is the mirage of constant activity in action. While you appeared busy, you failed to allocate your time and energy effectively to high-impact tasks that would have propelled you closer to your goals. Recognizing this mirage is the first step in breaking free from it and shifting your focus toward purposeful productivity.

THE VITAL ROLE OF DELEGATION AND AUTOMATION

Acknowledging that you can't do everything yourself is a crucial realization in both time management and successful prioritization. In fact, this lesson proved to be a pivotal turning point in my life as the founder of DJS Entertainment, my first business and one of Houston's hottest wedding entertainment and production firms.

In its early days, DJS Entertainment was a modest side hustle, with me working part-time as a DJ, taking on any gig that came my way, and barely scraping together $30,000 a year. The pivotal moment came when I decided to embrace automation. Digital contracts replaced cumbersome paperwork, automated invoices ensured timely payments, and a sophisticated email drip campaign was set up to convert new leads into paying clients. These changes not only streamlined operations but also freed up valuable time and mental energy.

BATTERIES NOT INCLUDED

However, the true game-changer was the automation of back-end tasks. Collecting wedding timeline information, musical preferences, and various event details necessary for the DJ's success was made effortless through automated systems. Customer service tasks that were once mundane and time-consuming now flowed seamlessly.

Furthermore, DJS Entertainment expanded its success by wisely delegating workload in the production department. We hired skilled individuals to handle the setup of sound and lighting, allowing our DJs to focus solely on what they excelled at – delivering remarkable performances and packing dance floors.

The results were nothing short of remarkable. In less than a year, DJS Entertainment transitioned from my humble side hustle grossing less than $30,000 annually to a thriving enterprise generating multiple six-figures in revenue. This transformation is a testament to the power of delegation and automation, demonstrating how they can turn a struggling endeavor into a flourishing success story.

Here's the real deal – I might have the skills to change the oil in my car or mow my lawn, but that doesn't mean it's the best use of my time. Think about it. I could spend a sunny Saturday with grease up to my elbows or pushing a lawnmower, but what if I used those hours to lock in a deal that could boost my business's profits? Or even better, what if I spent that time at the park, making my kids laugh and building memories? That's worth way more than what I'd shell out to someone to do the yard work for me.

> Delegation is like outsourcing the management of a portion of your time portfolio.

When I look at where my time goes, I've got to choose – do I spend it on something that just gets the job done, or do I invest in the richness of life, in the moments that really count? Buying back my time, so I can put it where it matters most, that's what it's all about. This is how I transformed DJS Entertainment and it's how I keep my life focused on what truly brings value and joy. It's not about just keeping busy; it's about making every hour count for something more.

THE IMPACT OF PURPOSEFUL PRODUCTIVITY

When we shift our focus from "doin' the most" to doing what truly matters, we unlock our potential for greater efficiency and fulfillment. Purposeful productivity is like a well-tuned engine – it runs smoothly, efficiently, and reliably. This entails dedicating our time and energy to tasks that align with our values, goals, and vision for the future.

> Purposeful productivity is like a well-tuned engine – it runs smoothly, efficiently, and reliably.

Consider a scenario where you have a project at work. Instead of succumbing to the urge to constantly check your email or engage in unimportant tasks, you dedicate focused, uninterrupted time to your project. The result is a higher quality output, completed in less time. This shift not only enhances your effectiveness but also brings a profound sense of purpose and satisfaction to your daily endeavors. It's like investing in a high-yield asset that pays dividends in the form of accomplishment and personal growth.

MINDFUL TIME MANAGEMENT

Mindfulness plays a significant role in transforming your approach to time management. Just as mindfulness in meditation involves being fully present and aware of the moment, mindful time management means being conscious of how you allocate your time and recognizing the difference between busyness and true productivity. It's like having a GPS for your time – it helps you navigate your day with purpose.

Imagine a day when you consciously set intentions for how you'll use your time. You pause to consider whether each task on your to-do list aligns with your larger goals. You practice self-awareness, noticing when you're tempted to engage in low-priority tasks that detract from your purpose. This mindful approach empowers you to make informed choices about how to spend your hours, ensuring that your time investment aligns with your values and objectives.

BREAKING FREE FROM THE EXCESSIVE HUSTLE

Breaking free from the "doin' the most" cycle is not a one-time event but an ongoing practice. It's similar to a fitness regimen – consistent effort leads to long-term results. This endeavor requires discipline and a commitment to maintaining focus on what truly matters. It's like sculpting a work of art; you refine your time management skills over time, chiseling away the excess until you reveal the masterpiece of a purpose-driven life.

Imagine embarking on this journey of self-improvement. You establish daily routines that prioritize high-impact tasks, delegate responsibilities where possible, and eliminate or automate low-priority activities. Over time, this practice becomes second nature, and you experience the cumulative benefits of increased productivity, enhanced fulfillment, and a more intentional, purposeful existence.

REFLECTIONS/TAKEAWAYS

As we conclude this chapter on prioritizing purposeful productivity and breaking free from doin' the most, take a moment to reflect on your own journey. Consider the following questions to help you assess any areas or tasks that might be hindering your productivity:

What are some specific instances in your daily life where you find yourself caught up in doin' the most, rather than focusing on tasks that truly matter?

....
....
....
....
....
....

Have you identified any low-hanging fruit tasks or mundane activities that you tend to use as a form of procrastination?

....
....
....
....
....
....

Are there any high-impact tasks related to your purpose or goals that have been neglected due to excessive busywork?

....
....
....
....
....
....
....
....
....

Have you attempted to delegate or automate tasks that could free up your time for more meaningful contributions?

....
....
....
....
....
....
....
....
....
....

How do you currently prioritize your daily activities? Are they aligned with your values and long-term vision?

....
....
....
....
....
....
....
....
....
....
....
....
....
....
....

Remember that the journey towards purposeful productivity is a continuous one. By reflecting on these questions and being mindful of your choices, you can take meaningful steps towards maximizing your efficiency and fulfillment in all aspects of your life.

FREE FROM SELF-DOUBT

Before we can embark on the journey of self-belief and purpose, we must first confront and dismantle the formidable barrier of self-doubt. In this chapter, we will embark on a transformative journey that involves challenging the negative self-talk that can subtly creep into our minds, practicing self-compassion when we falter, and surrounding ourselves with the uplifting influences that fortify our belief in our abilities.

SUBTRACT TO ADD: CREATING SPACE FOR GROWTH

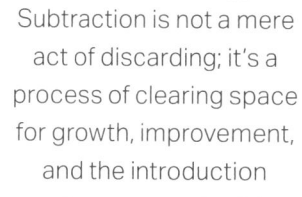

Subtraction is not a mere act of discarding; it's a process of clearing space for growth, improvement, and the introduction of more meaningful elements into our lives. Picture this as decluttering a room to make way for new furniture and decor that align with your style and purpose. Just as we cannot fill a cup already brimming to the top, our lives require openness and space for fresh possibilities. When our lives are cluttered with nonessential or energy-draining elements, there's little room for what genuinely matters. Learning to empty our cups, subtracting and releasing what no longer serves us, allows us to invite in the fresh, transformative, and purposeful.

> Subtraction is not a mere act of discarding; it's a process of clearing space for growth, improvement, and the introduction of more meaningful elements into our lives.

> Just as we cannot fill a cup already brimming to the top, our lives require openness and space for fresh possibilities.

CONFRONTING NEGATIVE SELF-TALK

Imagine your inner dialogue as a persistent critic who dwells in the shadows of your mind, casting doubt on your abilities and potential. It's time to turn the spotlight on this relentless critic and challenge its narrative. Consider this process as rewriting the story of your life. When you catch yourself thinking, "I can't do this," treat it as an inaccurate interpretation of your journey. Challenge this narrative by rephrasing your thoughts, affirming your abilities, and reminding yourself of past successes. Cognitive restructuring, akin to editing a story for clarity and accuracy, helps you identify and correct negative thought patterns. By actively engaging in this process, you gain mastery over your self-doubt, replacing it with a belief in your capabilities.

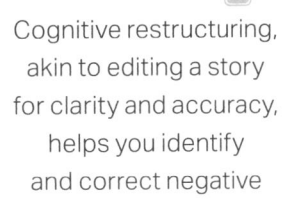

> Cognitive restructuring, akin to editing a story for clarity and accuracy, helps you identify and correct negative thought patterns.

SET REALISTIC GOALS

Setting realistic goals is like constructing a staircase to your dreams. Instead of attempting to leap straight to the top floor, you start with the ground floor and methodically ascend step by step. This approach not only makes your journey manageable but also ensures you can appreciate each accomplishment along the way, sort of like creating a map for your aspirations. Just as a builder measures and plans each step of a staircase, SMART goals are Specific, Measurable, Achievable, Relevant, and Time-bound. Breaking your aspirations into achievable milestones allows you to gradually accumulate evidence of your capabilities.

Each accomplished step chips away at self-doubt, making room for confidence to flourish.

SEEK SOCIAL SUPPORT

Social support acts as a safety net when self-doubt threatens to pull you down. Think of it as a lifeline extended by friends, family, or like-minded peers. Sharing your goals and aspirations with a supportive network is like seeking refuge during a storm. These individuals offer encouragement, perspective, and a sense of belonging. Research consistently underscores the importance of social support in bolstering self-esteem and resilience. Just as a community provides shelter and strength during adversity, engaging with a supportive network fortifies your belief in yourself and your journey, weakening the grip of self-doubt.

EMBRACE FAILURE AS A LEARNING OPPORTUNITY

Failure is like a sculptor's chisel, shaping your character and skills. Instead of dreading it, consider it an essential tool for personal growth. Many successful individuals faced numerous setbacks before achieving their goals. Embracing failure as a learning opportunity is comparable to becoming an apprentice in the workshop of life. Rather than fearing mistakes, view them as stepping stones on your path to mastery. Dr. Carol Dweck's research on the growth mindset emphasizes the importance of this perspective. Those who view challenges and failures as opportunities for

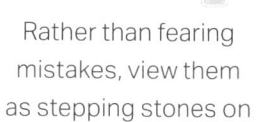

> Rather than fearing mistakes, view them as stepping stones on your path to mastery.

growth are more likely to persist and succeed. By adopting this mindset, you not only navigate setbacks with resilience but also nurture self-belief in your capacity to evolve and excel.

PRACTICE MINDFULNESS AND SELF-AWARENESS

Mindfulness and self-awareness are like mirrors for your thoughts and emotions. Engaging in mindfulness meditation is like holding up that mirror to observe your inner workings without judgment. It's the equivalent of watching a movie of your thoughts and emotions, detached from their immediate impact. Mindfulness-based interventions, with their focus on the present moment, have been associated with increased self-esteem and reduced self-criticism. By cultivating self-awareness and the ability to observe self-doubt objectively, you regain control over your self-image and beliefs. This mindful approach empowers you to challenge and reshape self-doubt, ultimately paving the way for greater self-belief.

> Mindfulness and self-awareness are like mirrors for your thoughts and emotions.

CELEBRATE ACHIEVEMENTS

Celebrating achievements is like depositing coins in your self-worth bank. Each accomplishment, no matter how small, contributes to your self-esteem and reinforces a positive self-image. Think of it as adding pearls to a necklace; each pearl represents a success or milestone. By consciously acknowledging your achievements, you string together a beautiful necklace that symbolizes your journey of growth and accomplishment. Positive reinforcement and self-praise are the thread that weaves this necklace. When you appreciate your successes, you reinforce your self-worth and resilience against the corrosive effects of self-doubt.

SEEK PROFESSIONAL HELP WHEN NEEDED

Seeking professional help is like enlisting a skilled guide when navigating uncharted territory. Just as you would hire an expert to help you navigate a challenging hike, consulting a therapist or counselor can provide valuable guidance and support when self-doubt significantly impacts your mental health and productivity. Therapy, especially cognitive-behavioral therapy (CBT), offers a structured approach to challenging and overcoming self-doubt. Much like a seasoned guide, a therapist can help you navigate the terrain of your thoughts and emotions, equipping you with the tools and insights needed to dismantle self-doubt's hold on your life. It's a courageous step toward a more confident and purposeful existence.

As we embark on the journey of freeing ourselves from self-doubt, remember that belief is the key to unlocking your true potential. The path to purpose and fulfillment requires us to confront and conquer self-doubt, allowing belief to flourish. In the chapters that follow, we will explore the power of faith, the next step in our quest to power our purpose and fuel our future. By applying these evidence-based strategies and drawing inspiration from those who have successfully overcome self-doubt, you'll pave the way for enhanced productivity, increased self-worth, and a more confident pursuit of your aspirations.

REFLECTIONS/TAKEAWAYS

Before we wrap up this chapter, take a moment for introspection. The journey to being FREE from self-doubt requires self-awareness and reflection. Here are some self-reflective questions to help you navigate this transformative path:

What negative self-talk patterns do you frequently notice in your thoughts?

> *Identifying these patterns is the first step in challenging and changing them.*

....
....
....
....
....
....

How do you typically react to setbacks or failures?

> *Reflect on whether you view them as learning opportunities or as confirmation of your self-doubts.*

....
....
....
....
....
....

Who are the individuals in your life who offer you unwavering support and encouragement?

> Consider how you can nurture these relationships and seek their guidance during challenging times.

What goals or dreams have you hesitated to pursue due to self-doubt?

> Write them down and commit to taking small, actionable steps toward them

In what ways can you practice self-compassion when you make mistakes or encounter difficulties?

> Think of how you would comfort a friend in a similar situation and apply that kindness to yourself.

Do you have a mindfulness, prayer, or meditation practice?

> If not, consider starting one to enhance self-awareness and reduce self-criticism

What recent achievements or milestones have you overlooked or downplayed?

Take a moment to celebrate them, no matter how small they may seem.

Have you ever considered seeking professional help or guidance to address self-doubt?

Reflect on whether it might be a valuable step in your journey.

Remember, the path to self-belief and purpose is unique for each of us. Use these questions as a starting point to explore your own experiences, challenges, and aspirations. In doing so, you'll continue to make strides toward a life fueled by belief in your abilities and a clear sense of purpose.

3

FAITH TO FLY!

> "Faith is taking the first step even when you can't see the whole staircase."
> —Dr. Martin Luther King Jr.

Growing up, I was a basketball fanatic. I played every chance I got, watched countless basketball movies, studied shooting technique videos, and even slept with my basketball beside me. But let's get one thing straight: I'm not one of those guys who looks back and applies an Instagram filter to their memories, exaggerating their glory days. I was good – not the best, but I could certianly hold my own. I fit the stereotype of a white kid who couldn't jump, dunk, or sprint exceptionally fast. My ball-handling skills were decent, but my jumper – now that was a force to be reckoned with. I could shoot the lights out from anywhere on the court, having practiced and perfected my shot daily. Players like Steve Kerr, Reggie Miller, and Ray Allen – essentially anyone who could effortlessly shoot from the three – were my idols.

I share all this not to brag about my basketball skills, but to set the stage for a larger conversation about faith and the power of belief. Beyond mastering shooting techniques like BEEF (balance, eyes on the target, elbow in, and follow through), one of the most pivotal aspects of becoming a great shooter is visualization. I had to see the ball swishing through the net even before releasing it from my fingertips. This principle isn't just limited to basketball; it applies universally. It might sound clichéd, but if you really want to achieve something, you have to truly believe in it. Belief is potent, transcending mere hope and being more forceful than a simple wish.

Belief is like the wind beneath our wings, propelling us to new heights and uncharted territories. Again…another cliché and kind of cheesy, but it's true! It's the wind that allows our wings to soar through the skies! Just like the wind, our faith is unseen. You can't see the wind, but you can feel its impact. You can even see its effect on things like how it causes trees to move. Our faith in dreams and visions of the future is unseen but has a major impact on our present actions that bring the unseen into reality. It's that unwavering faith in our abilities, our dreams, and the path we've chosen to follow, much like my basketball days when I had to believe that every shot I took would find its mark. Belief is the driving force that makes the seemingly impossible possible.

> Belief is the driving force that makes the seemingly impossible possible.

THE VISUALIZING POWER OF BELIEF

In those countless hours spent on the basketball court, I learned that belief extends far beyond mere confidence. It delves into the realm of visualization, where success takes shape in your mind long before it becomes a reality. As I stood on that court, I had to envision every shot I took gracefully swishing through the net, not as a mere hope but as an unshakable certainty.

This principle of unwavering belief is exemplified in the story of Michael Jordan, the GOAT (we can argue that later! Lol). Jordan wasn't just confident; he possessed an unyielding belief in his abilities. He visualized making game-winning shots in the most pressure-packed moments. His mind painted a picture of success that he then translated into reality on the court. Jordan's belief in himself, is what fueled his relentless work ethic, and transformed him into one of the greatest basketball players of all time, winning numerous NBA championships and leaving a lasting legacy.

THE LIMITLESS POTENTIAL OF BELIEF

This power of belief is not confined to the realm of sports; it permeates every aspect of our lives. Whether you're pursuing a career, embarking on a personal journey, or striving to make a difference in the world, unwavering belief can be your guiding light, your North Star or compass. It's about seeing the future you desire in vivid detail and taking the necessary steps to turn that vision into your reality.

BELIEF VS HOPE

Belief isn't a passive hope; it's an active force that compels us to take action. When we truly believe in something, we're more likely to put in the effort, practice diligently, and persevere through setbacks because we know, without a doubt, that we can achieve it. Take Mark Zuckerberg, for instance. He didn't set out to connect the entire world; he started with the modest goal of connecting Harvard students through Facebook. His belief in the idea grew as the platform expanded to millions of users worldwide.

> Belief isn't a passive hope; it's an active force that compels us to take action.

Belief isn't constrained by the boundaries of reality; it's what allows us to push those boundaries and explore the unknown. It's what drove explorers to venture across uncharted seas, inventors to create groundbreaking technologies, and artists to express their innermost thoughts and emotions. Belief is the spark that ignites innovation and propels us forward.

BATTERIES NOT INCLUDED

While hope is a beautiful emotion, belief goes beyond it. Hope is like casting a wish upon a star, while belief is knowing that you are the architect of your destiny, and everything aligning in your favor. It's a conviction that you can shape your future, no matter how audacious your dreams may be.

> Hope is like casting a wish upon a star, while belief is knowing that you are the architect of your destiny, and the stars are aligning in your favor.

This chapter isn't just about the theory of belief; it's about providing you with practical strategies to strengthen your belief system. By practicing visualizing your goals as already achieved, like Olympic athletes who often visualize their perfect performance before the actual event, you'll build belief in your ability to achieve success. Surrounding yourself with supportive individuals who believe in you and your dreams, like Steve Jobs did when he surrounded himself with a team that shared his belief in the potential of personal computing, can be contagious and empowering. Creating positive affirmations that reinforce your belief in yourself and your goals, just as Muhammad Ali did when he declared himself the greatest, can build your confidence. And by starting with small, achievable goals, like Mark Zuckerberg's initial aim to connect Harvard students through Facebook, you'll see that each success builds your belief in your abilities and paves the way for larger accomplishments.

DAVID SETTLE

SPEAK WHAT YOU SEEK UNTIL YOU SEE WHAT YOU SAID!

Nobody embodies this idea of believing things into existence, and living a life fueled by faith better than François Mignon, author of the best-selling book 'Made from Scratch- finding success without a recipe.'

During an interview we did together François recited the following quote: "Speak what you seek, until you see what you've said!" This profound philosophy became the driving force that fueled her journey. At a time when she had only five dollars to her name, struggling to keep the lights on and make ends meet for her family, François didn't succumb to despair. Instead, she embraced the unseen power of belief and began to speak her aspirations into existence.

She spoke of success, abundance, and prosperity until those words manifested as her reality. With unwavering faith, she transformed that five dollars into over 5 million cupcakes sold, creating a thriving business empire. François Mignon's story serves as a shining example of the incredible impact faith can have when coupled with determination and action.

In the end, faith is the force that transforms ordinary individuals into visionaries, dreamers into doers, and challenges into triumphs. It's the power that allows us to rise above adversity and reach for the stars. So, as you embark on this journey of harnessing the power of your beliefs, always remember: If you believe it, you can achieve it!

REFLECTIONS/TAKEAWAYS

As we conclude this chapter on the power of faith to fuel our futures, let's engage in some thoughtful self-reflection to help you cultivate and harness the strength of your own belief system. Belief, as we've discovered, is not a passive state of mind but an active force that propels us toward our goals. Here are some prompts and statements to encourage your engagement:

Can you vividly see yourself living the life you aspire to? How does this visualization inspire you to take action in your life?

Visualization: *Take a moment to envision your most cherished goals and dreams*

How can these affirmations reinforce your confidence and motivation on a daily basis? Are there specific affirmations that resonate with you already?

Affirmations: *Consider creating positive affirmations that resonate with your beliefs and aspirations.*

Who are the individuals who genuinely support your dreams and believe in your abilities? How can you nurture these relationships to further empower your own belief system?

Surround Yourself:
Reflect on the people in your life

How have these experiences contributed to your personal growth and belief in yourself? What self-compassionate practices can you adopt to navigate future challenges?

Self-Compassion:
Think about the setbacks and challenges you've faced on your journey.

What are some achievable steps you can take today to start building your belief in your abilities? How do these small successes contribute to your overall confidence?

Small Steps: *Identify small, manageable goals that align with your larger aspirations.*

Remember, the path to self-belief and purpose is unique for each of us. Use these questions as a starting point to explore your own experiences, challenges, and aspirations. In doing so, you'll continue to make strides toward a life fueled by belief in your abilities and a clear sense of purpose.

4

FORCE
TO SUCCEED

"Nothing works unless you do."
—Maya Angelou

So far, we've explored three powerful batteries: Focus, Freedom, and Faith. Each of these batteries has charged you with the energy needed to propel you towards your purpose. But now, as we approach the next battery, it's time to unveil the true catalyst for success, the FORCE that makes everything possible.

As we've journeyed through Focus, we've learned the art of directing our attention with laser-like precision. Freedom has liberated us from self-imposed limitations, and Faith has fortified our belief in ourselves and our dreams. These batteries have prepared us for one essential truth: the real power is in the ACTION we take.

NOTHING WORKS BUT WORK

Let's be clear; "Force" is just another word for "work." *I just wanted to keep the iteration going and with all the words starting with 'F' lol)*. There's no magic formula or shortcut. Success doesn't come wrapped in a shiny package; it's the result of deliberate, consistent, and hard work. Force encompasses the determination to push through challenges, the resilience to bounce back from setbacks, and the work ethic to stay committed when the going gets tough.

> Success doesn't come wrapped in a shiny package; it's the result of deliberate, consistent, and hard work.

THE LAW OF MOTION

In the vast and expansive universe, stars and planets orbit, comets blaze trails, and galaxies spiral, all governed by the immutable laws of physics. The same laws that oversee the grand ballet of celestial bodies are at work in our mundane, everyday lives. Sir Isaac Newton's profound observation, encapsulated in his laws of motion, lays down the principle that an object at rest stays at rest, and an object in motion continues in motion, unless acted upon by an external force. Just as a spacecraft requires a rocket's thrust to break free from Earth's gravitational pull, we too need a significant force or drive to push beyond our comfort zones and reach new heights.

Imagine a boulder sitting at the top of a hill. It has all the potential energy it needs to race down the hill, yet it remains motionless. Why? Because potential alone isn't enough. It requires a push, a force, to transform its potential into kinetic energy. Similarly, our dreams, no matter how grand or noble, remain mere dreams without the force of action.

There's a well-known tale of a sculptor who, after carving a beautiful elephant from a block of stone, was asked how he did it. He responded, "I simply chipped away everything that wasn't the elephant." But even his chipping required force. The repeated, intentional strokes to bring his vision to life. Likewise, to carve out our destinies, to manifest our dreams, we need to chip away at our challenges, our fears, and our procrastinations, with deliberate and sustained force.

There's an inertia to life, a resistance to change. Every artist faces the blank canvas, every writer the blank page, every entrepreneur the daunting challenges of starting up, and every dreamer the abyss of the unknown. To move from a standstill, we must generate a force that overcomes this inertia. That force is our passion, our dedication, our work ethic, and our relentless drive.

Just as wind propels the sails of a ship, we need the winds of determination, resilience, and grit to power our journey. But remember, even the mightiest ship requires a captain's intent to set its course. It's crucial to realize that we have a significant role to play in our destiny, and our actions, our force, steer the ship of our life's journey.

> We are the captains of our fate, and our actions, our force, steer the ship of our life's journey.

So, as you contemplate your ambitions, dreams, and desires, know that wishing them into existence is just the beginning. It's the unwavering force of action, the commitment to move when everything else remains static, that truly turns potential into reality. The universe operates on the principle of force, and so should we. Nothing works but work. Your dreams are waiting; all they need is the force to succeed.

EMBRACING THE HEAT: FROM GOOD TO GREAT

Follow me for a moment, and don't mind me... underneath all the tattoo's I'm a true science and math geek! I actually taught middle school math, algebra, geometry and integrated physics and chemistry for a few years. It's truly fascinating stuff!

In the intricate dance of molecules, heat plays the pivotal role of a choreographer. When heat is applied, it stirs up molecules, causing them to move faster and more vigorously. This accelerated movement is what triggers changes in the state of matter. A once solid ice block, when warmed, turns into flowing water, and with continued heating, that water is transformed into rising steam.

This tangible metamorphosis offers a profound analogy for our own life journeys. Just as matter requires heat to change states, we often require challenges — our life's 'heat' — to stir us up and catalyze our transformation. While the warmth of comfort can keep us in a consistent, unchanging state, it's the heat of adversity, challenge, and growth that propels us forward, pushing us from our status quo.

Heat, in its essence, is a form of energy. And when introduced to our lives, it doesn't always feel comfortable. It can be the pressure of deadlines, the weight of responsibilities, or the intensity of personal struggles. But just as molecules dance and change their state with heat, these heated moments in our lives, though uncomfortable, have the power to reshape us, refine our goals, and redirect our paths.

So, when faced with the 'heat' of life, remember that it's an opportunity to transform from good to great. Challenges, pressures, and the occasional burns are simply nudges, urging us to evolve, adapt, and rise. Let the heat refine you, let it mold you, and let it lead you towards a state of greatness. After all, without heat, there's no change, and without change, there's no growth.

Embrace the heat, and watch yourself transcend states, from good to unequivocally great.

FROM POTENTIAL TO POWER: HARNESSING THE FORCE WITHIN TO FORGE AHEAD

I vividly recall a conversation with one of my mentors and heroes, Dr. Eric Thomas, the world's number one motivational speaker. During our discussion, he imparted a powerful insight that profoundly transformed my approach to execution:

'The possibility of future success is the enemy to absolute success right now?'

These words struck a chord, revealing that the mere possibility of future success can paradoxically hinder our current progress. It keeps us in a state of hope, wishful thinking, and waiting, all without taking meaningful action. However, when we summon our inner force, combine it with unwavering faith, and channel it into diligent work and effort, that's when our future success manifests in the present. The future is merely a concept until we actively shape it into our reality. As someone once wisely remarked, 'The only way to predict the future is to create it!'

> The future is merely a concept until we actively shape it into our reality.

Procrastination, doubt, and distractions will always be lurking. But the power of Force lies in your ability to overcome these obstacles. Look to the stories of those who have succeeded against all odds. They didn't possess superhuman abilities; they simply

BATTERIES NOT INCLUDED

put in the work. They were determined to make progress each day, to keep the momentum alive.

So, what's the path forward? It's simple but not easy. It's about showing up consistently, even when you don't feel like it. It's about setting clear goals, developing a disciplined routine, and embracing challenges as opportunities for growth. Force is not about exerting unnecessary pressure; it's about harnessing your inner drive and taking intentional action.

In the end, nothing works but work. The force of your determination, the power of your resilience, and the strength of your work ethic will determine your success. As we close this chapter and this book, remember that your dreams are within reach, but only if you're willing to put in the work.

> The force of your determination, the power of your resilience, and the strength of your work ethic will determine your success.

Embrace the power of Force as the driving energy behind your purpose. Fuel your future with relentless effort, and you'll discover that success is not a matter of chance; it's a matter of choice. Choose to work for your dreams, and you'll find that nothing is impossible. Your journey has just begun, and with the Force as your guide, there's no limit to what you can achieve.

May the Force be with you (I couldn't help myself! Lol) as you power your purpose and fuel the future you've always dreamed of.

REFLECTIONS/TAKEAWAYS

As we conclude this journey, take a moment to reflect on the following questions:

What dreams and goals have you been postponing or hesitating to pursue?

....
....
....
....
....
....
....
....

How has this book reshaped your perspective on work and the power of consistent effort?

....
....
....
....
....
....
....
....

Now, let's turn reflection into action. List three concrete steps you can take right now to get closer to your goals. Remember, small actions accumulate into significant results. Commit to taking these steps and harness the force within you:

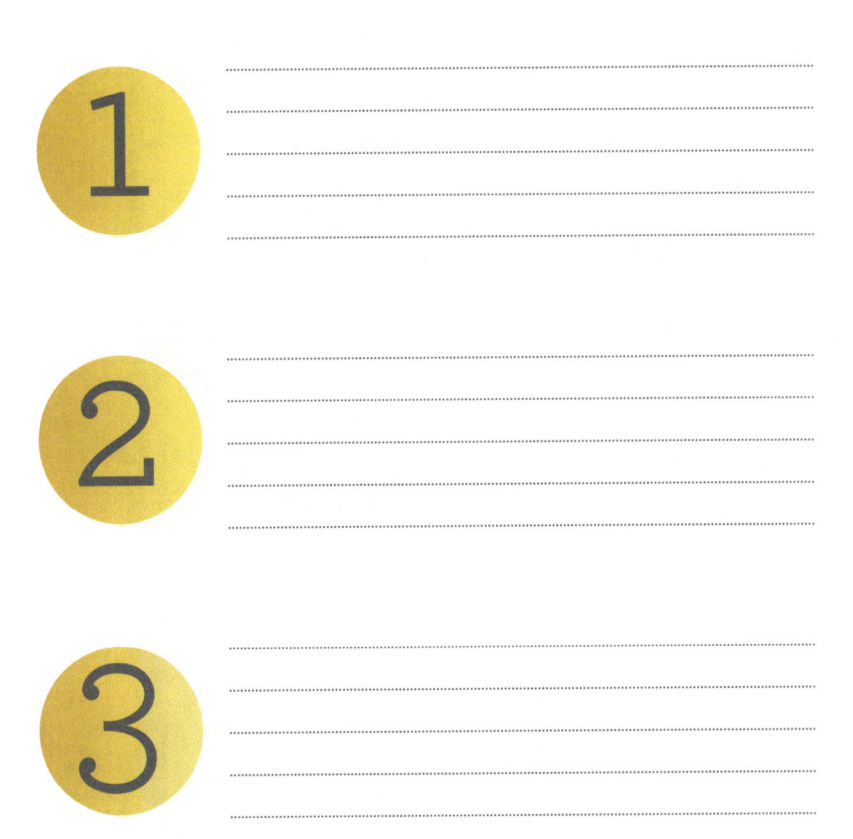

1. ....
....
....
....

2. ....
....
....
....

3. ....
....
....
....

Embrace the power of Force as the driving energy behind your purpose. Fuel your future with relentless effort, and you'll discover that success is not a matter of chance; it's a matter of choice. Choose to work for your dreams, and you'll find that nothing is impossible. Your journey has just begun, and with the Force as your guide, there's no limit to what you can achieve.

Batteries Not Includes | David Settle

FUN
THE FUEL OF FULFILLMENT

"Success is not the key to happiness. Happiness is the key to success. If you love what you are doing, you will be successful."

—Albert Schweitzer

Just when you thought we were done, here's one more battery to jolt your journey – Fun! Why Fun? Because at the end of the day, if we're not having fun, then what's the point? We've talked about Focus, Freedom, Faith, and Force, but now let's turn our attention to the overlooked yet essential ingredient of a successful and fulfilling life – Fun.

> At the end of the day, if we're not having fun, then what's the point?

THE SCIENCE OF FUN

You might be wondering, "Is fun really that important?" The answer, backed by scientific research, is a resounding yes. Numerous studies in psychology and neuroscience have shown that having fun and enjoying life can significantly impact your success and well-being.

Research reveals that fun activities trigger the release of endorphins, your brain's feel-good chemicals, which not only reduces stress but also enhances your mood and resilience, making it easier to tackle challenges. Moreover, engaging in enjoyable activities stimulates your brain's creative centers, fostering innovative thinking. Fun also strengthens relationships by facilitating positive connections with others, which can be invaluable for personal and professional success.

THE JOURNEY OF FUN

The process of achieving your dreams should be enjoyable, not just the end result.

Success is often associated with reaching specific goals, but what about the journey itself? The process of achieving your dreams should be enjoyable, not just the end result. Here's why:

Studies demonstrate that people who enjoy the process are more likely to stay motivated and persistent. Fun acts as a continuous source of energy, driving you toward your goals. Furthermore, fun and enjoyment in your work lead to increased productivity, as passion fuels effort. Fun-loving individuals tend to bounce back from setbacks more easily; they see challenges as opportunities to learn and grow, a hallmark of successful people.

Fun acts as a continuous source of energy, driving you toward your goals.

LIVE, LAUGH, SUCCEED

It's not just about the destination; it's about the journey. It's about living in the moment, creating memories, and having fun along the way. Success should be joyful, not joyless. So, how can you incorporate more fun into your life?

ACTION STEPS

FIND YOUR JOY

Begin by identifying activities that genuinely bring you joy and happiness. Reflect on the moments in life when you felt truly alive and content. It might be a hobby, a passion, or a simple daily ritual. Once you've pinpointed these sources of joy, make a commitment to incorporate them into your daily routine. Whether it's reading a good book, spending time in nature, or practicing a creative art, these moments of joy will infuse your life with positivity and make each day more enjoyable.

CELEBRATE SMALL

One's success is not solely defined by grand achievements but also by the small victories along the way. Take time to recognize and celebrate your accomplishments, no matter how modest they may seem. Whether you completed a task that's been on your to-do list or made progress toward a larger goal, acknowledging these small wins adds an element of fun and motivation to your journey. It's a reminder that every step forward is worth celebrating.

SHARE LAUGHTER

Laughter is a powerful and universal language of joy. Surround yourself with people who bring laughter into your life. Seek out friends and companions who share your sense of humor and make you laugh. Laughter is not only contagious but also a potent stress reliever. It fosters strong connections and deepens relationships. By sharing laughter with others, you not only enhance your own well-being but also create a joyful and supportive network that will uplift you on your path to success.

EMBRACE PLAY

Life is an adventure, and it's essential not to take it too seriously. Allow yourself to play, explore, and try new things. Embracing playfulness adds a sense of spontaneity and curiosity to your life. It encourages you to step out of your comfort zone and discover new experiences. Whether it's trying a new sport, exploring a new hobby, or simply approaching challenges with a playful mindset, infusing playfulness into your life will make the journey more exciting and enjoyable. Remember, the more you embrace play, the more you'll relish the ride toward your goals.

The more you embrace play, the more you'll relish the ride toward your goals.

To wrap things up, Fun is not an indulgence but a necessity for success and fulfillment. It fuels your passion, creativity, and resilience, making your journey more enjoyable and your goals more attainable. So, as you continue to power your purpose and fuel your future, don't forget to infuse it with the magic of Fun. Live, laugh, and succeed.

REFLECTIONS/TAKEAWAYS

As we conclude this journey and explore the battery of "Fun," take a moment to dig deep within yourself. What brings you joy? What activities genuinely make you happy? It's time to uncover the passions that light up your life.

Consider the following:

Activities You'd Do for Free: Think about the things you'd do without expecting any payment or recognition. These are the activities that come from the heart, driven solely by your passion and enjoyment.

Free Time Pursuits: Imagine you have a day entirely free of obligations. What would you choose to do with that time? Picture yourself engaged in activities that excite you and make you smile.

Means and Accessibility: Reflect on the things you can go out and enjoy right now, without worrying about financial constraints, budgets, or time constraints. These are the accessible sources of joy that are within your reach.

> By identifying these sources of genuine enjoyment, you're taking a significant step toward infusing your life with fun. Make a commitment to prioritize these activities, whether they involve creative pursuits, outdoor adventures, quality time with loved ones, or simply moments of solitude that bring you peace. Embracing what truly makes you happy will not only enhance your journey but also fuel your success and fulfillment.

As you continue your path to powering your purpose and fueling your future, remember that success is not just about reaching your goals; it's also about living a life filled with joy and moments that make your heart sing. So, go ahead, explore your passions, chase your dreams, and never forget to add a dash of fun to every step of the way. Live, laugh, and succeed.

ALL CHARGED UP: POWERING YOUR PURPOSE, FUELED BY FOCUS, FAITH, FREEDOM, FORCE, AND FUN

Now that we are all charged up, we can conquer anything! Fully equipped with the batteries of focus, faith, freedom, force, and, of course, fun, we have all the energy we need to power our purpose and fuel our future. These batteries collectively fuel your transformative journey towards success and fulfillment, empowering you to conquer any challenge that lies ahead.

In "Focus," we honed the art of directing our attention, cultivating laser-like precision in our pursuits. We learned that focus is not only a skill to be developed but also a key that unlocks the transformative potential within us.

"Freedom" was the catalyst for embracing authenticity and living in alignment with our values. We broke free from self-imposed limitations, realizing that true freedom begins from within.

"Faith" was our guiding star, instilling unwavering belief in our abilities and dreams. We uncovered the power of resilience and self-assurance, proving that what we believe in ourselves ultimately shapes our reality.

"Force," our penultimate battery, reminded us that nothing works but work itself. Determination, resilience, and a strong work ethic fueled our journey, taking us from dreams to tangible results.

And then, the surprising twist: "Fun." We discovered that, amidst all the hard work and focused determination, embracing joy and playfulness is not only delightful but essential for success. Fun breathed life into our journey, making the process as meaningful as the destination.

As you close this chapter and this book, remember that success is not only about achieving goals but also about living a life filled with passion, authenticity, and laughter. It's about embracing the power of focus, the strength of faith, the liberation of freedom, the determination of force, and the pure joy of fun.

So, what's your next step on this incredible journey? Reflect on the lessons learned, the wisdom gained, and the action steps that beckon you. Embrace your newfound focus, faith, freedom, force, and fun, and let them guide you toward a future where success is not just a destination but a joyful, purposeful, and fulfilling way of life.

Thank you for joining me on this transformational voyage through "Batteries, Not Included." May your path be illuminated by the light of focus, faith, freedom, force, and fun as you power your purpose and fuel your future. With these batteries fully charged, there's no limit to what you can achieve.

Made in the USA
Columbia, SC
07 January 2024